# HEAD

Curated by Robert Curcio and
D. Dominick Lombardi

**BOSI** CONTEMPORARY
July 10 – August 11, 2013

Front cover: Ronald L. Hall, *Blind Nation*, 2010, oil on canvas, 30 x 40 in. (detail)
Design: BOSI Contemporary
Text editing: Kara Brooks

ISBN: 9781304140227

# CONTENTS

7   CURATORIAL STATEMENT

EXHIBITED WORKS
12   *CHRISTOPHE AVELLA BAGUR*
16   *BENEDETTA BONICHI*
20   *RICHARD BUTLER*
24   *LORI FIELD*
28   *RIEKO FUJINAMI*
32   *CHAMBLISS GIOBBI*
38   *RONALD L. HALL*
42   *NINA LEVY*
48   *D. DOMINICK LOMBARDI*
52   *ESTHER NAOR*
56   *LENA VIDDO*

61   CONTRIBUTORS

63   ACKNOWLEDGMENTS

6

# CURATORIAL STATEMENT

The portrait, as with the still life and landscape, has been a standard fundamental form in the visual arts for many centuries. Mostly through the Modern Era, the artist has focused on their subject's inner turmoil, political views, fame and fortune, social place, religious beliefs and esthetic values to offer a more encompassing version of the human condition. Today, a few artists have moved even farther away from the traditional portrait. Hence, most previously employed means of identifying an individual have been replaced with a far more emotional or psychological symbolism.

HEAD is an exploration of a physical object, a locus of the personal, contemporary open-ended concepts and concerns. As a result, the wide-ranging and diverse depictions of HEAD in this exhibition present a more universal message. Somewhat identical in their generic appearance, the HEAD has received a serial treatment of deconstruction to its basic bits and parts. Elements are dislocated, deconstructed then rebuilt to amplify the activity below the surface.

Here, after careful consideration, recognition slowly begins to emerge that the HEAD is now a pivotal narrative element that hinges upon many paths. Consciously or unconsciously, some part of the viewer is reflected in the HEAD leading them to a new sort of odd, uncomfortable intimacy. While the individual physical resemblance has been dislocated, the psychological underpinnings have been rebuilt and amplified. The HEAD is now seen as more of an abstracted self-portrait, but of whom?

**Christophe Avella-Bagur's** merging of adults and children through emotional and situational swings of the human condition are a direct commentary on cloning, biotechnologies and globalism. Here, the HEAD becomes a seat for multiple presentations as it floats and searches for its right place in a post-human world.

Using x-ray technology and detailed representations of human skeletons, **Benedetta Bonichi** more than suggests vanity, as well as the sexual act of 'giving' HEAD. Since Bonichi literally shows us the bare bones in her digital prints there is an unmistakable connection to mortality and death, and perhaps the afterlife – or so we hope.

**Richard Butler** veils his HEADs behind, what can be described as patterns from industry and religion. In *bubblegirl*, we see a HEAD obscured by jumbo-sized bubble wrap. The sight of a woman's HEAD encased in suffocating plastic is truly alarming, while the apparent calm of the 'victim' is oddly settling, and may give the viewer a sense of overcoming a fear. In *smallconfessional* Butler questions the spiritual usefulness of the necessity to confess one's sins, as if the judgment of god is the only thing that should guide ones morality.

**Lori Field**'s painted and collaged hybrids of animals and humans have their HEADs filled and layered with imagery that further entrenches their otherness. As a result, they find their humanity and identity through the narratives they share with the viewer and not through common features.

**Rieko Fujinami** addresses the transient elements of identity to reveal the soul inside the HEAD. Her amorphous pigment washes and touches of detail can barely hold on in an atmosphere veiled with interference and abstraction, while the memory of a face – the specific identifier of a HEAD – leaves us with a link to a life once lived.

**Chambliss Giobbi**'s personalized constructed HEADs are obsessive and psychological – a compression of moments. The fragmented HEAD that Giobbi rearranges can lead to any multitude of facial features acquiring an aspect of desire or identity in ways that owe little or nothing to the origins of those elements.

Political views come to the fore in the work **Ronald L. Hall**. Any politician will tell you that perception trumps reality, as this 'reality' does not escape the gaze of Hall. Being critical, especially as a visual artist, is essential to continuing a vital and thought provoking dialogue and Hall aims at the ultimate bullseye – truth.

The HEADs in **Nina Levy**'s sculptures and photographs challenges our notion of scale. The drastic changes in the relative sizes of her HEADs evoke an emotional response, while the meaning behind those changes incites fantasy. The narratives also have some basis in what we experience when we sleep where the slightest tweak in a daily routine can become a big part of that same evening's dreamscape.

**D. Dominick Lombardi** sees the HEAD more as an open-ended receptacle than a symbol in and of itself. It's a place where information can enter and educate, enlighten, entertain or arouse as long as we let it. It's an overused cliché, but life is a journey and that journey begins and ends in the HEAD.

Reminiscent of an amusement game in one piece and classic animal rugs in another, **Esther Naor** hints at autobiography, but her minimal bright yellow heads with plumb red lips reach a narrative beyond vulnerability, beauty and death.

Fantasy plays a role in the HEADs of **Lena Viddo**. Here, delicate portrayals of naughty nubiles instill in the viewer a distinct feeling of uneasiness as their stare entices. What lingers in that discomfort is the fear that as you gaze at that beautiful HEAD, there lurks something dangerous and sinister.

For this exhibition, we have stated a new message of iconic vocabulary as we creep even farther into the complexities of the HEAD as a central fixation – a symbol of something greater than itself. We have looked at artists who present the HEAD as a container of memory, thought and intelligence – an emotional center that controls, creates and contends at will, awake or asleep, young or old, with everything that comes its way. We see the HEAD as a beacon of untamed energy and desire – an igniter of fantastical visions – or a symbol of life itself.


Robert Curcio
D. Dominick Lombardi

June 2013

# EXHIBITED WORKS

# CHRISTOPHE AVELLA-BAGUR

On an ethereal ground of white light Avella-Bagur shows us archetypal representations of male and female bodies that answer our expectations of mass-produced perfection. Avella-Bagur disrupts this ideal with a second layer of portraits painted in visceral flesh-tones that never quite register with the face's outline. The two portraits are collapsed together to create disturbingly distorted juxtapositions painted in the grotesque manner of El Greco or Goya. Christophe Avella-Bagur gives us an uncompromisingly contemporary kind of painting, which while remaining firmly figurative presents a fresh look at the complex nature of human identity as depicted by the virtual world. Born in 1968 in Avignon, France, Avella-Bagur's paintings have been extensively exhibited in French museums and art centers, as well as European and Asian art fairs.

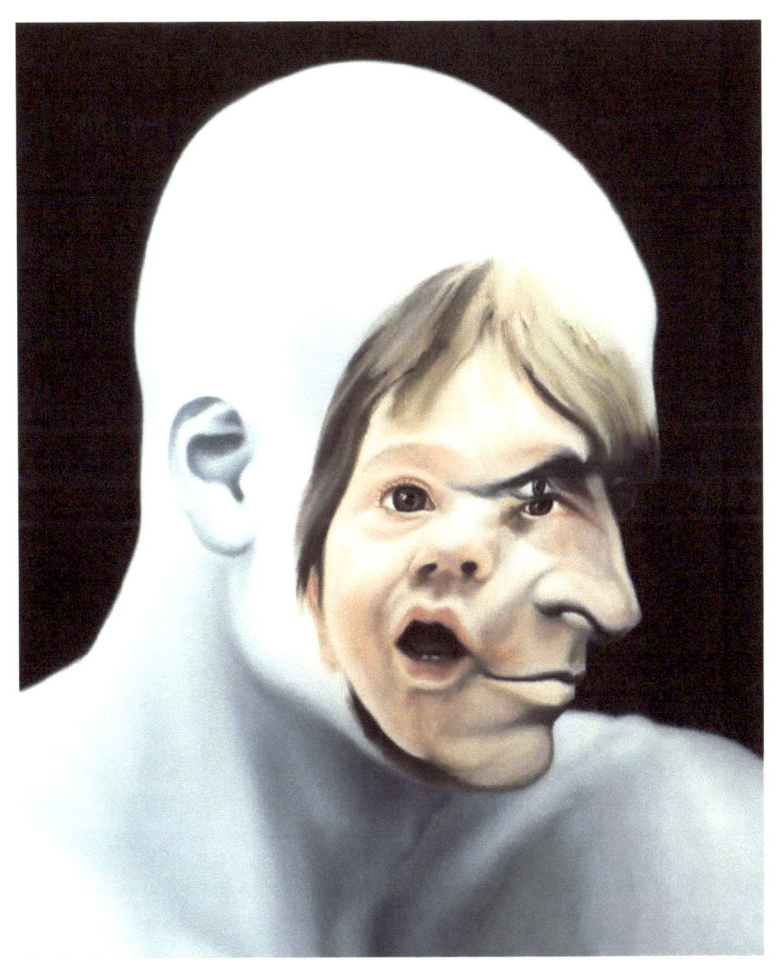

***Face Fs Still Child***
2012
oil on canvas
23 ⅔ x 19 ⅔ in.

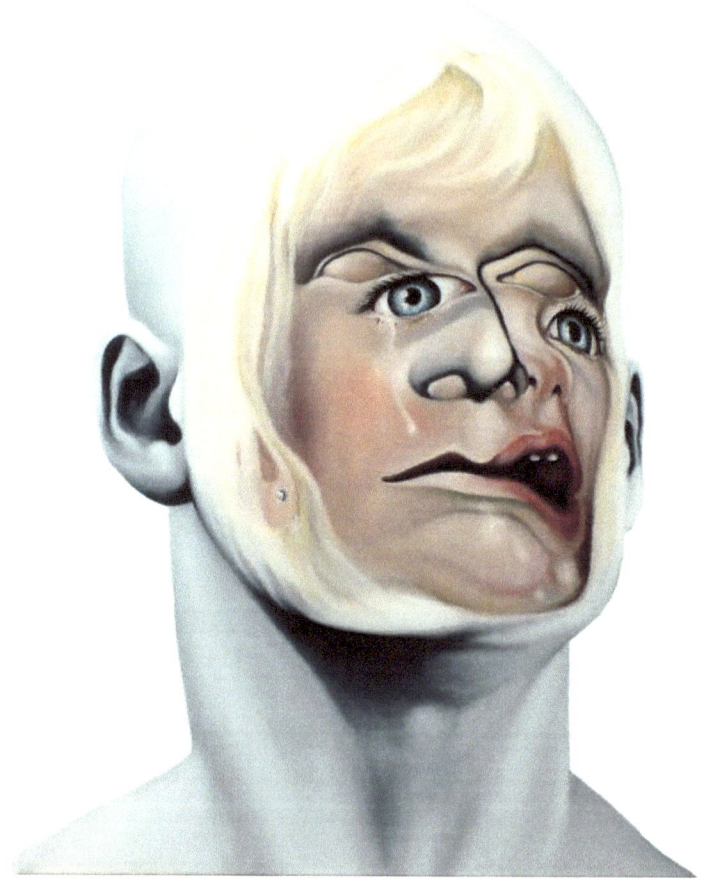

***FACE FS STILL CHILD 2***
2012
oil on canvas
23 ⅔ x 19 ⅔ in.

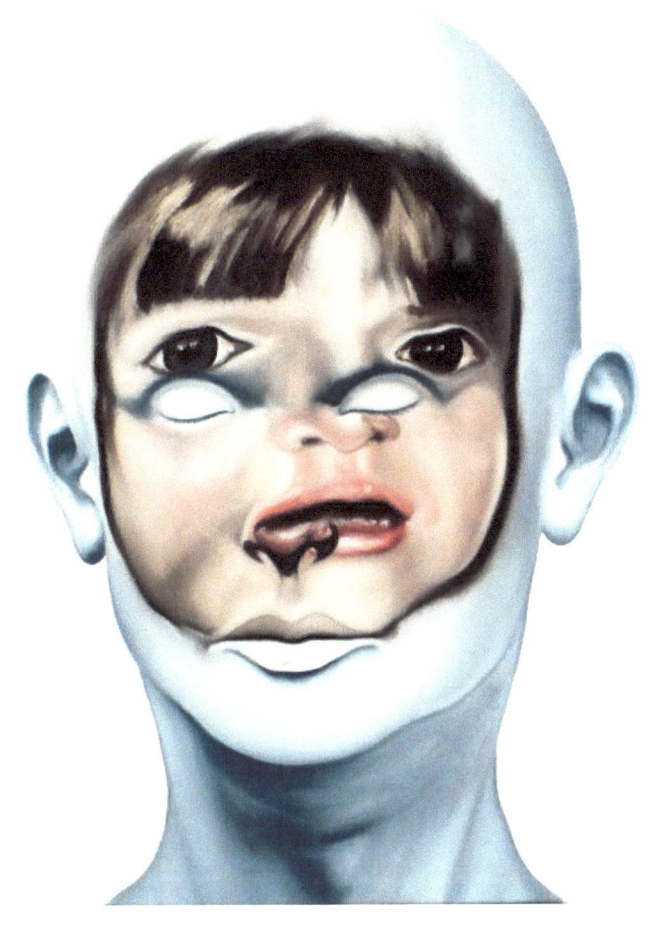

**FACE FS STILL CHILD 3**
2012
oil on canvas
23 ⅔ x 19 ⅔ in.

# BENEDETTA BONICHI

Benedetta Bonichi was born in 1968 in Italy. She worked in her family's atelier since she was four. Bonichi studied music, Romance languages, anthropology, Greek history and archaeology. She started exhibiting in 2002. Bonichi's works are in permanent collections of museums including the MAC (São Paulo), the MACRO (Rome), the Pharos Trust Foundation (Cyprus) and Centro Wilfredo Lam (Havana).

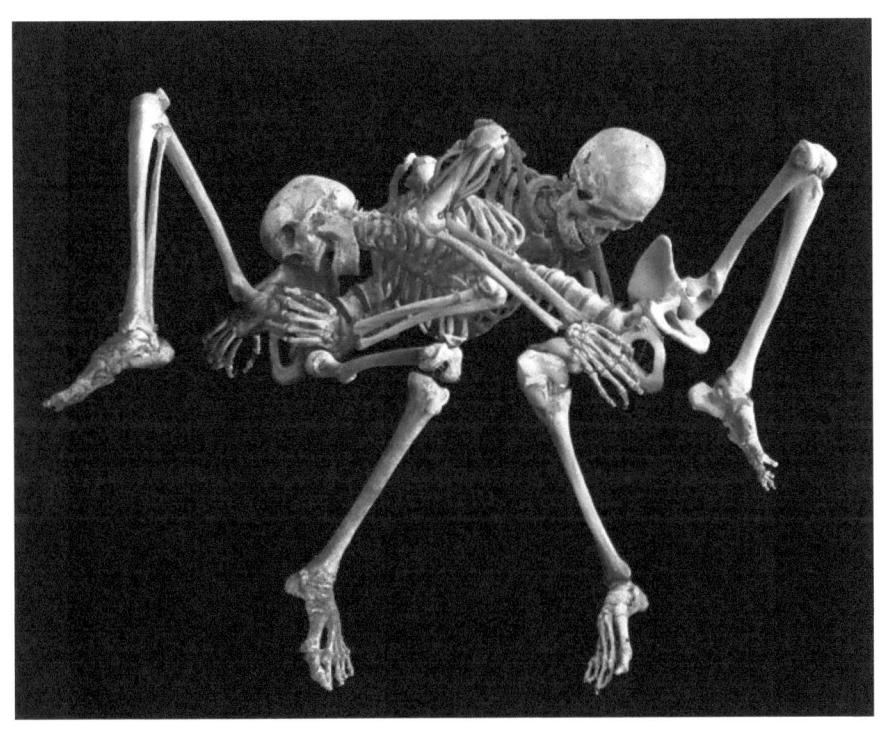

***ESSAYS IN LOVE: LA RECHERCHE [K179]***
2009
mixed technique on paper
23 ⅔ x 31 ½ in.
11/12 +2a.p.

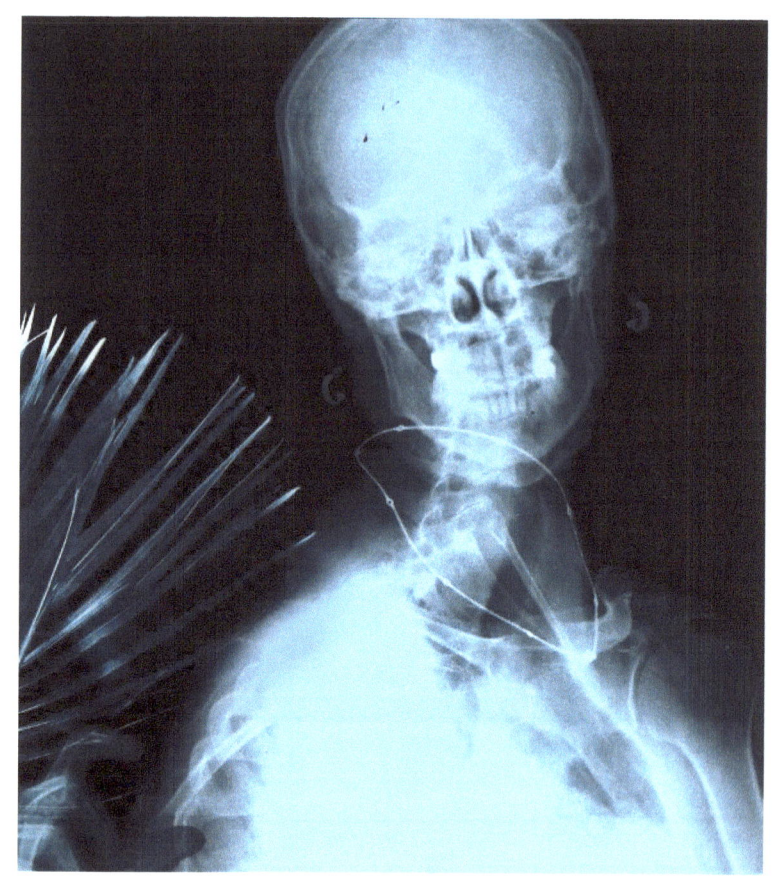

**DONNA CON VENTAGLIO [K200B]**
2011
mixed technique on alu – dibond
19 ¾ x 20 ⅞ in.
2/3 +2 a.p.

RICHARD BUTLER

Richard Butler was born in Hampton Court England. He studied painting at the
Epsom School of Art and Design. Fifteen years ago, after a successful career as
founder and singer/songwriter for the rock band The Psychedelic Furs, Richard
returned to painting. He lives and works in New York.

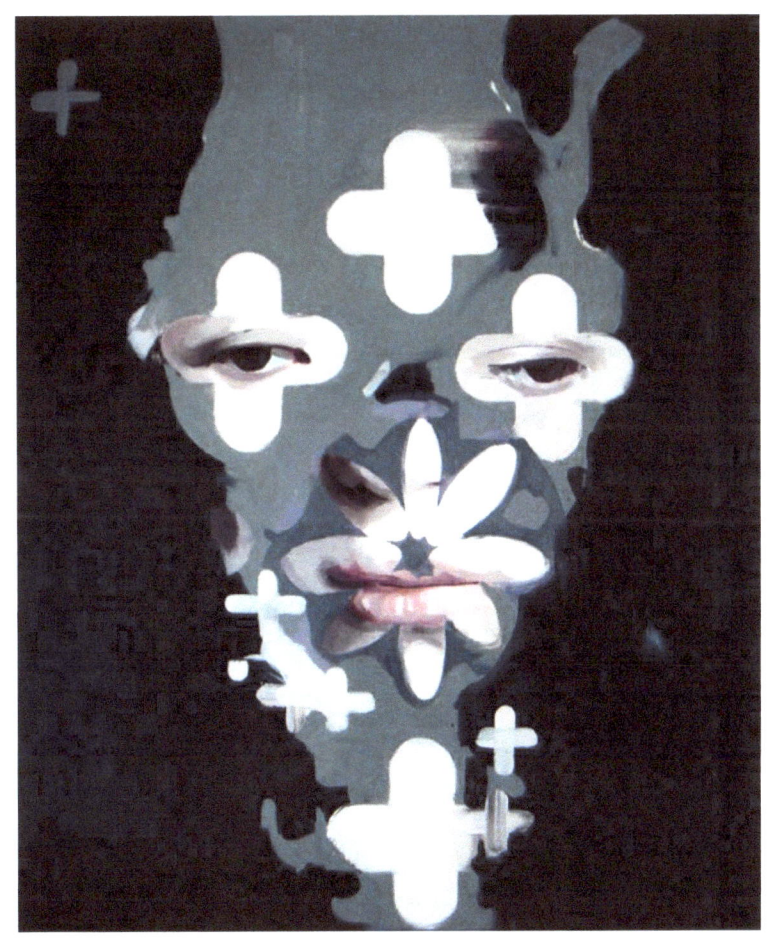

**SMALLCONFESSIONAL**
2011
oil on canvas
30 x 26 in. (frame included)

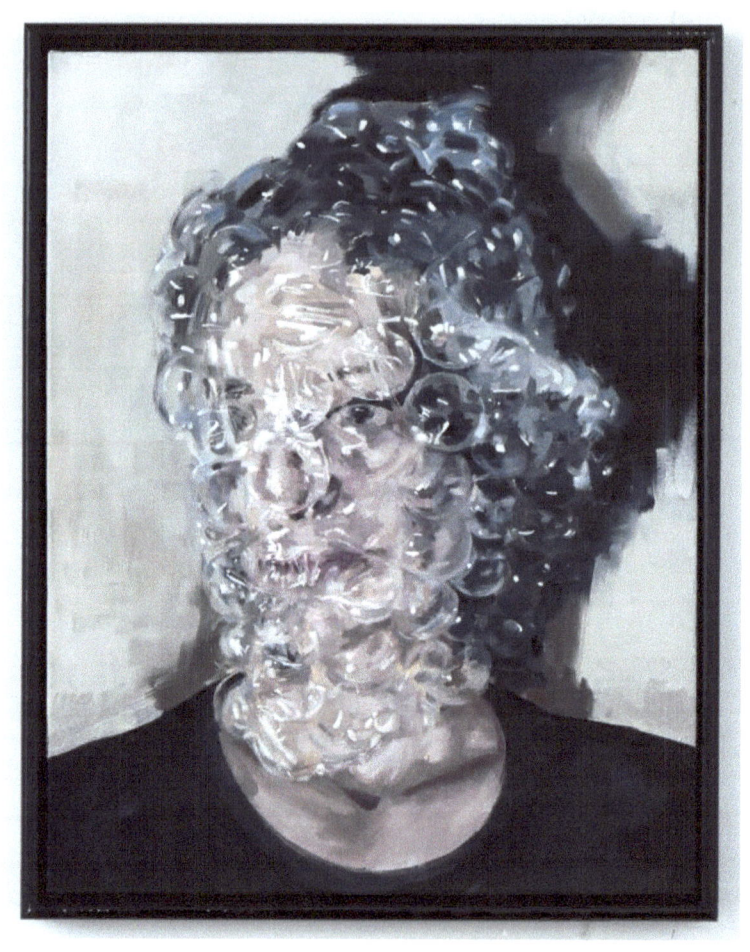

***BUBBLEWRAP***
2010
oil on canvas
32 x 26 in. (frame included)

22

## Lori Field

Lori Field is primarily a self-taught artist. She exhibits her work regionally, nationally, and internationally in many group and solo exhibitions. Her paintings have been exhibited at the Outsider Art Fair in New York City as well as in the New Jersey Fine Arts' Annual Cultural Exploration at the Morris Museum, Morristown, NJ. Field also teaches courses in mixed media drawing and collage at Montclair Art Museum's Yard School of Art, Montclair, NJ, and encaustic painting workshops at her home studio. She also enjoys curating group exhibits.

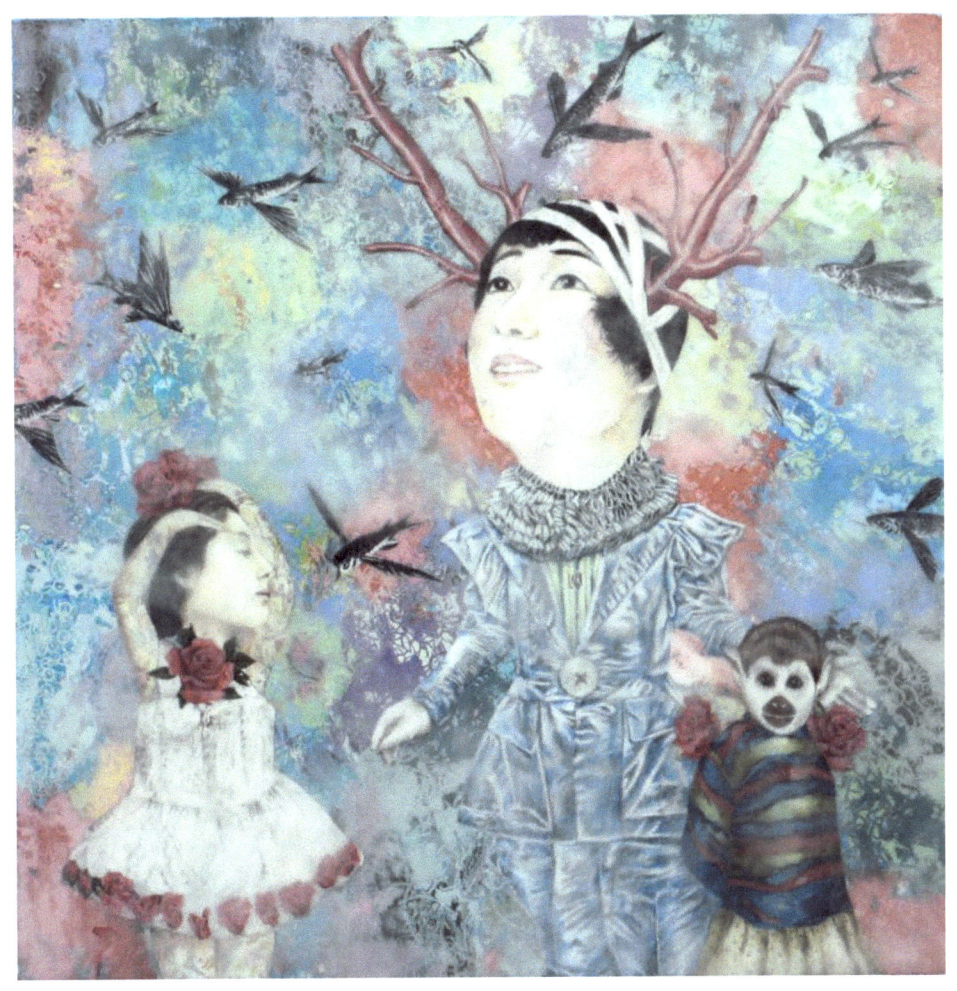

**SVENGALI**
2008
colored Pencil Mounted on Wooden Panel with Encaustic
16 ¼ x 12 x 1 in.

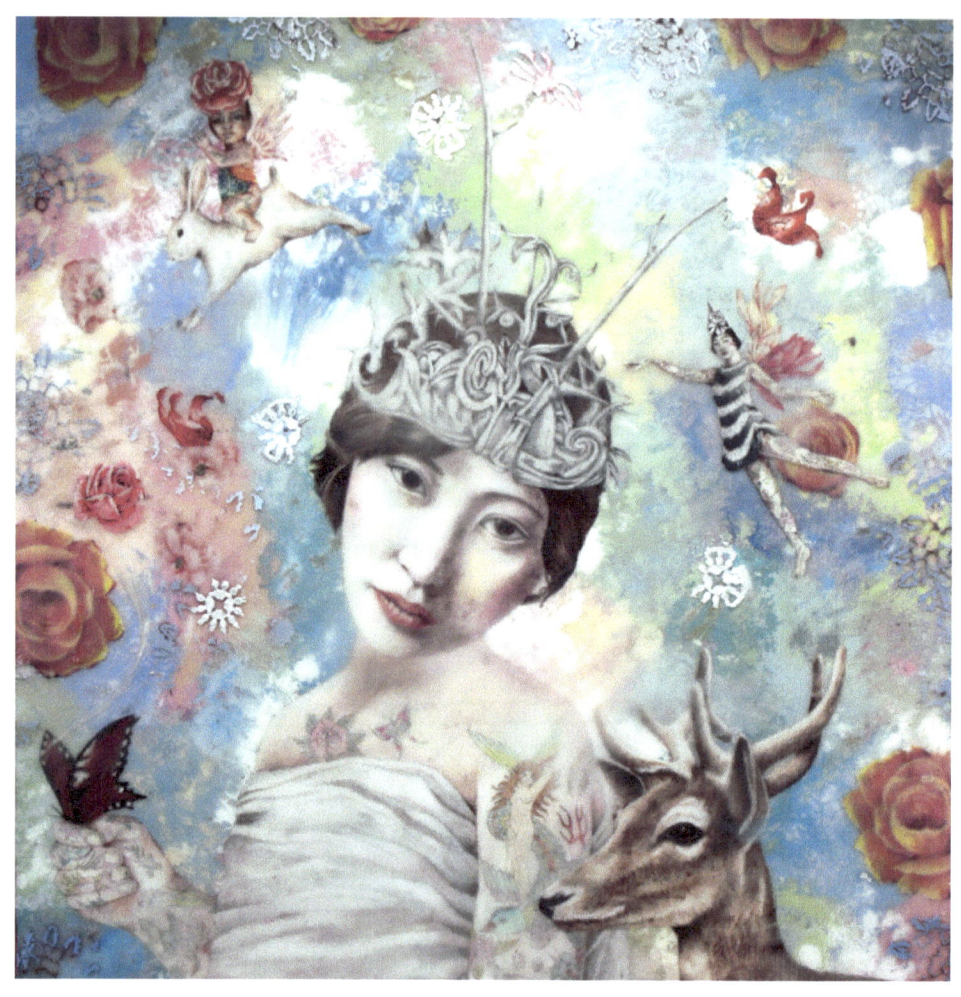

***BE-CAREFUL***
2008
colored Pencil Mounted on Wooden Panel with Encaustic
20 x 20 x 2 ½ in.

26

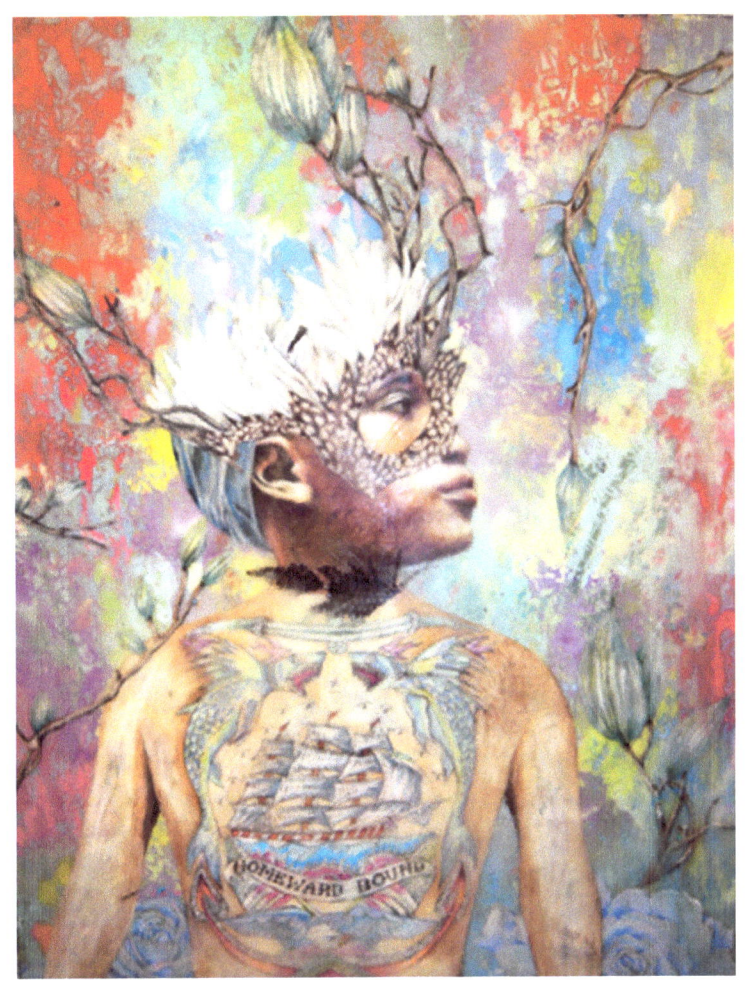

### HOMEWARD BOUND
2008
colored Pencil Mounted on Wooden Panel with Encaustic
20 x 16 x 1 in.

# RIEKO FUJINAMI

Rieko Fujinami's diverse range of media includes etching, copper tempera, frottage/drawing, fresco secco, drawing on clear film and acrylic mirror, glass painting, digital collage and video.

She has had over 60 one-person exhibitions in Japan and the United States. Fujinami's art is featured in a number of public collections including the Japan National Museum of Modern Art (Tokyo), the Japan Railway Art Museum (Tokyo), the Tikotin Museum of Japanese Art (Haifa), and the Kanagawa Prefectural Museum of Modern Art (Hayama-machi). Fujinami currently works and resides in Beacon, NY.

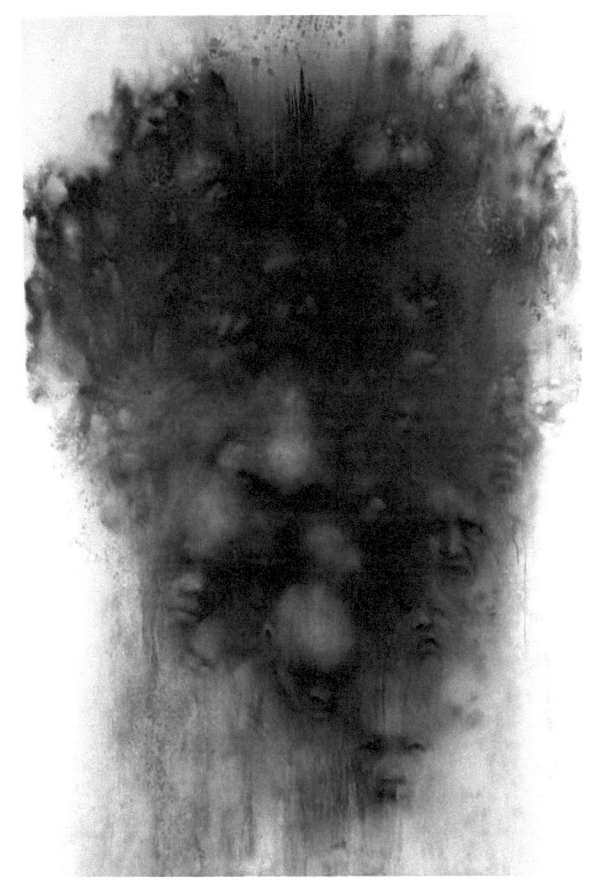

***BLACK RAIN - TRIUMPHANT LAUGH***
2008
Drawing on clear film, dry pigment and acrylic color
60 x 40 in.

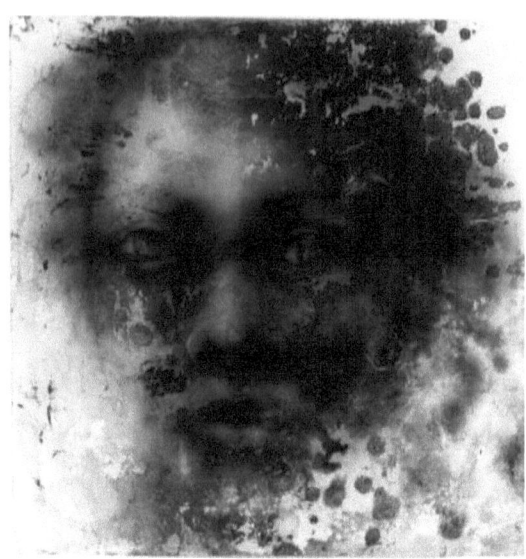

**CW-DCE-06**
2006
drawing on clear film mounted on mirror
20 x 20 in.

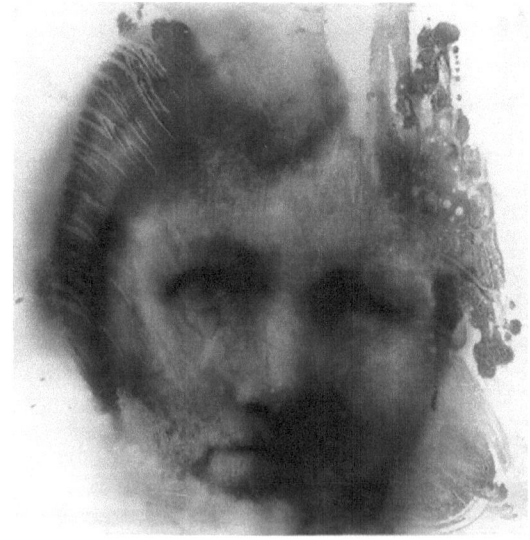

**An-Jan-06**
2006
drawing on clear film mounted on mirror
20 x 20 in.

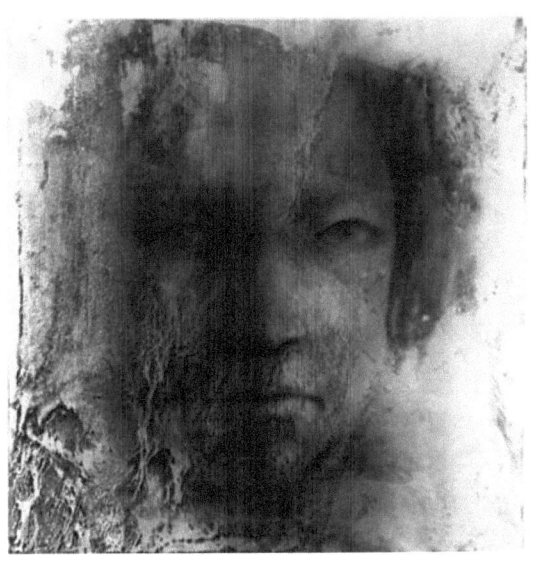

**Mi-Jan-06**
2006
drawing on clear film mounted on mirror
12 x 12 in.

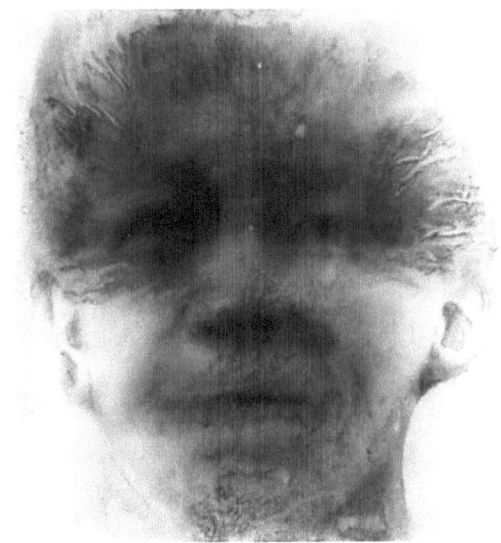

**AD-Jan-06**
2006
drawing on clear film mounted on mirror
12 x 12 in.

# CHAMBLISS GIOBBI

Chambliss Giobbi grew up in Katonah, New York and received a B.F.A. in Music Composition from Boston University. A recipient of Guggenheim, NEA and NYFA fellowships, Giobbi was a prolific composer of classical music before turning to visual art.

Giobbi has exhibited in numerous museum shows, including the National Portrait Gallery, (D.C.), The Katonah Museum of Art, (Katonah, NY), The Oakland University Art Museum, (Detroit, MI), The Kohler Art Center, (Sheboygan, WI), The National Academy Museum, (NYC), The Islip Art Museum, (Islip, NY), and is in the permanent collection of the Museo De Bellas Artes in Santander, Spain. He lives and works in New York City.

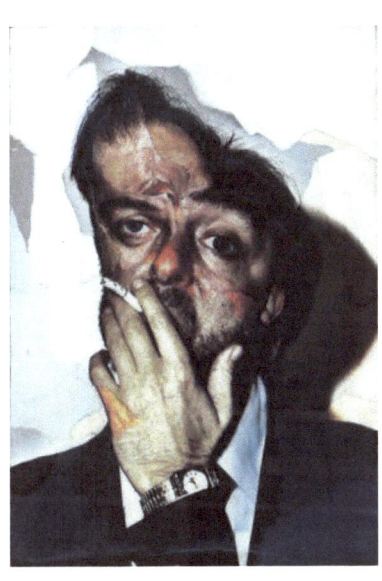

### *TINY PORTRAIT OF FISHER STEVENS 1*
2013
Collage, Bees Wax on Masonite
7 x 5 in.

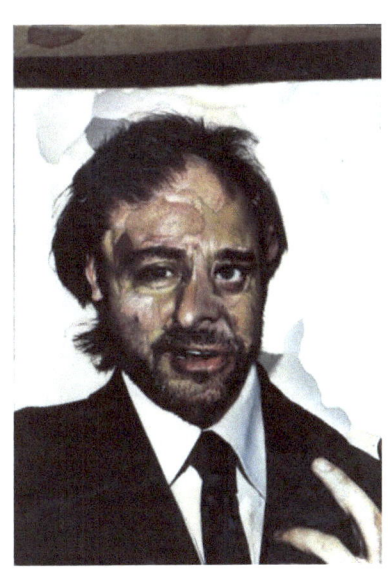

### *TINY PORTRAIT OF FISHER STEVENS 2*
2013
Collage, Bees Wax on Masonite
7 x 5 in.

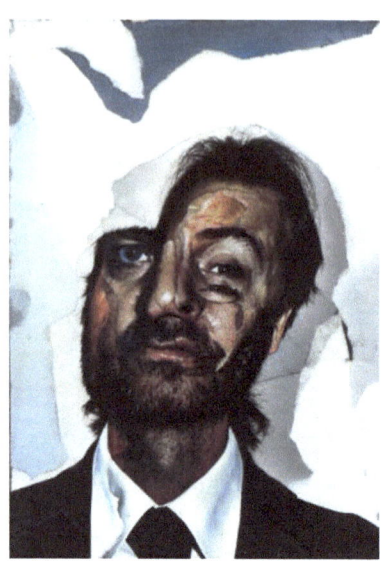

### *TINY PORTRAIT OF FISHER STEVENS 3*
2013
Collage, Bees Wax on Masonite
7 x 5 in.

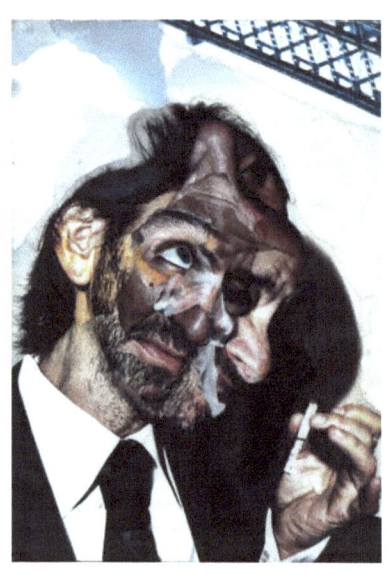

### *TINY PORTRAIT OF FISHER STEVENS 4*
2013
Collage, Bees Wax on Masonite
7 x 5 in.

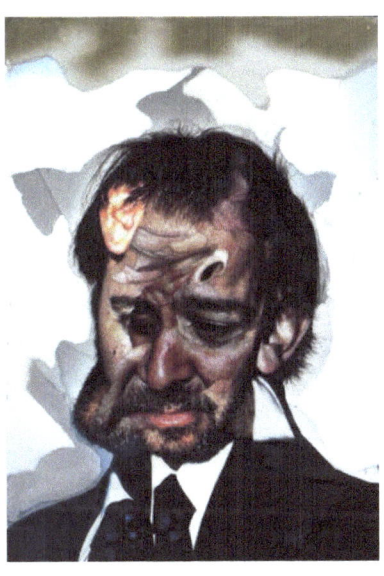

### *TINY PORTRAIT OF FISHER STEVENS 5*
2013
Collage, Bees Wax on Masonite
7 x 5 in.

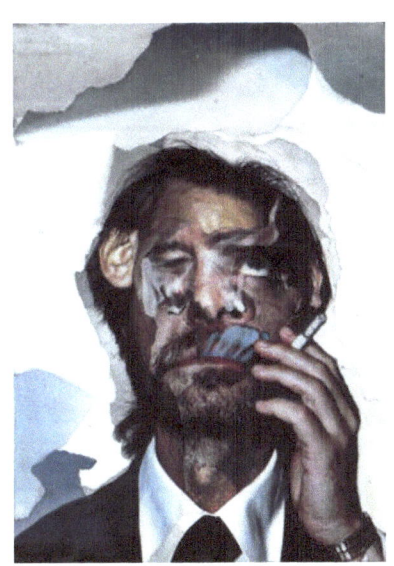

### *TINY PORTRAIT OF FISHER STEVENS 6*
2013
Collage, Bees Wax on Masonite
7 x 5 in.

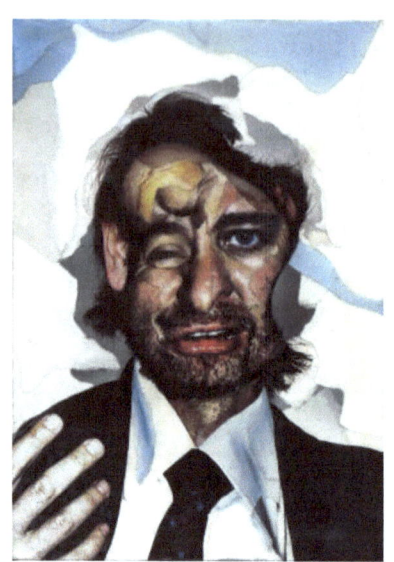

**_TINY PORTRAIT OF FISHER STEVENS 7_**
2013
Collage, Bees Wax on Masonite
7 x 5 in.

# Ronald L. Hall

"The experience of growing up as a young artist amidst the crime ridden neighborhoods of Pittsburgh Pennsylvania helped me to realize that art should be a tool for learning and for teaching. I attempt to demonstrate through my art, my interpretation of historical and contemporary issues with an emphasis on race and identity in America. To demonstrate, through my art, the injurious effects of visual representations and misrepresentations in society and how it effects people's perception of one another in terms of race, physical appearance or social status is the ultimate goal."

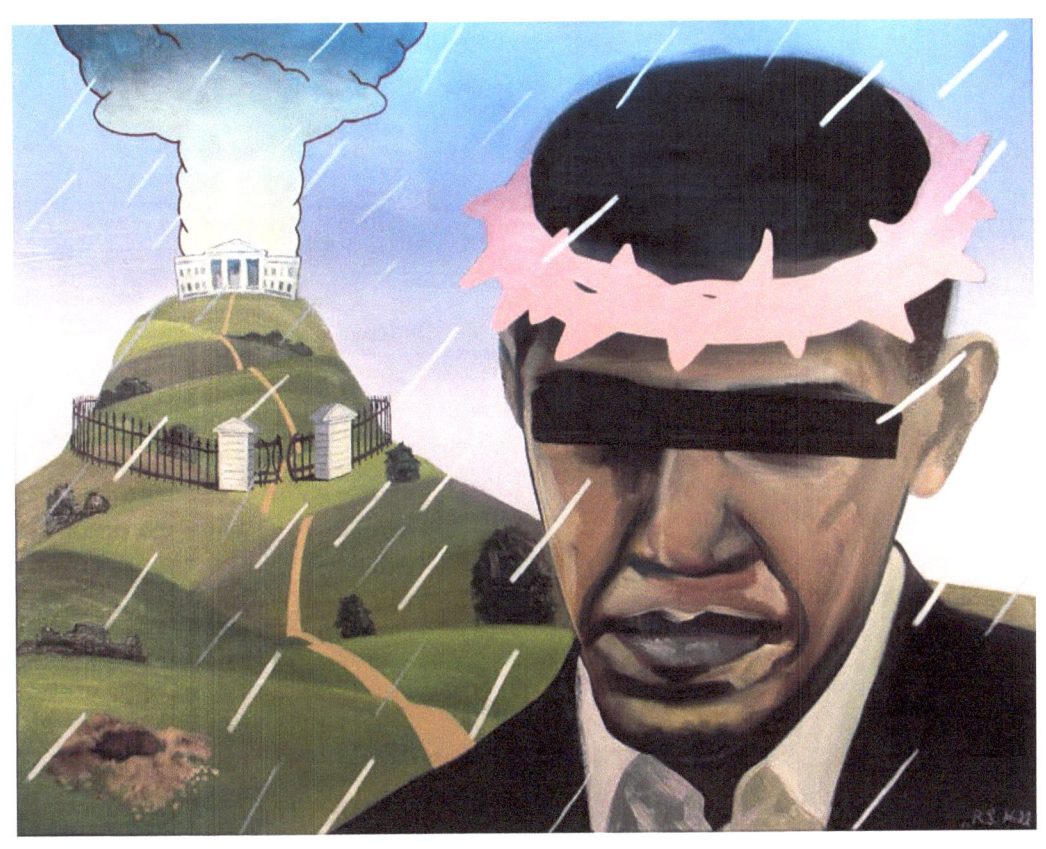

***BLIND NATION***
2010
oil on canvas
30 x 40 in.

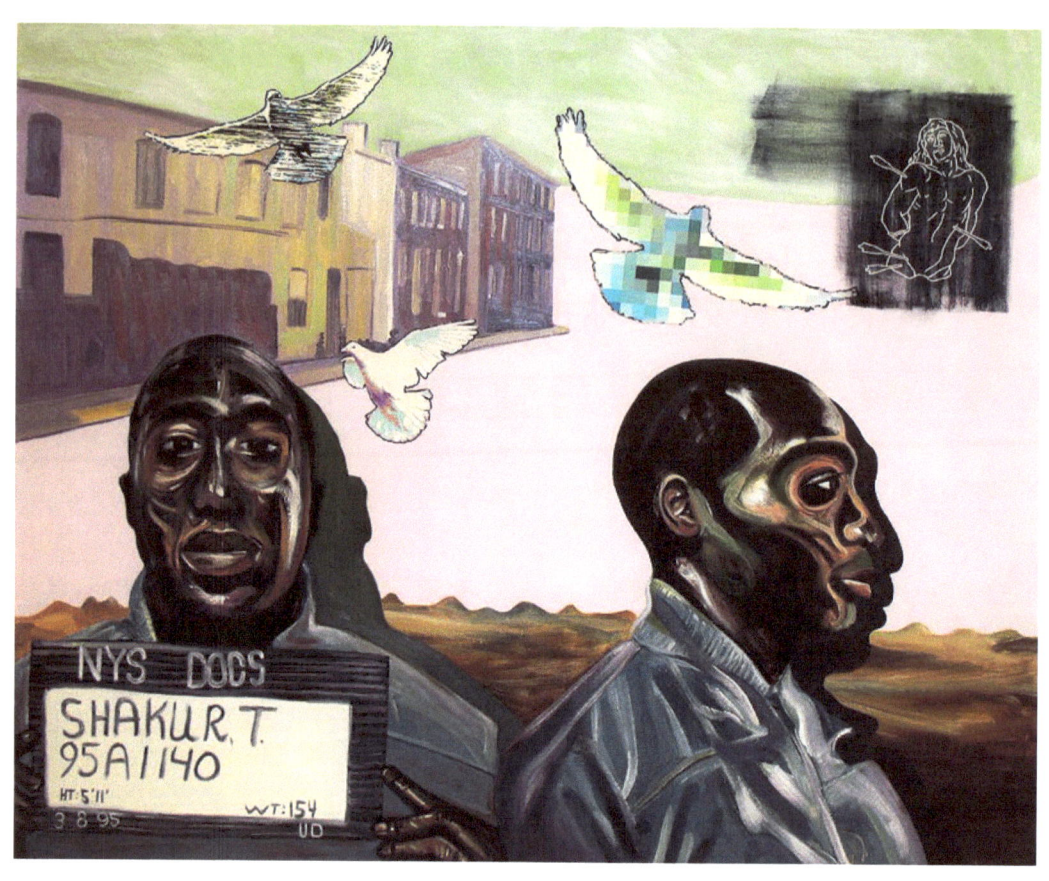

**THE MARTYR OF DEATH ROW**
2010
oil on collage on canvas
48 x 60 in.

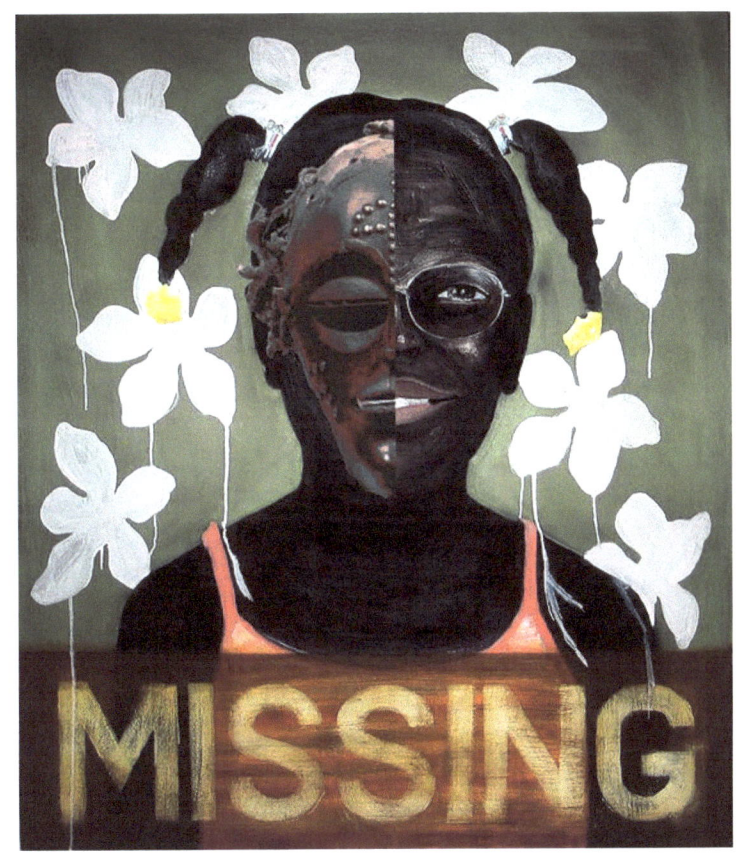

**MISSING PART 4**
2007
oil & collage on canvas
42 x 35 in.

# NINA LEVY

Nina Levy was born in Los Angeles in 1967. She has a BA in English and Art from Yale University, and an MFA from University of Chicago. Levy has exhibited her sculpture and photographs in various venues including The National Portrait Gallery in D.C., The DeCordova Museum, The Aldrich Contemporary Art Museum, the Museum of Contemporary Art in San Diego and the Brooklyn Museum. This fall, Levy will teach a course at the New York Academy of Art on the head in sculpture, focusing on art history and studio practice. She now lives and work in Brooklyn.

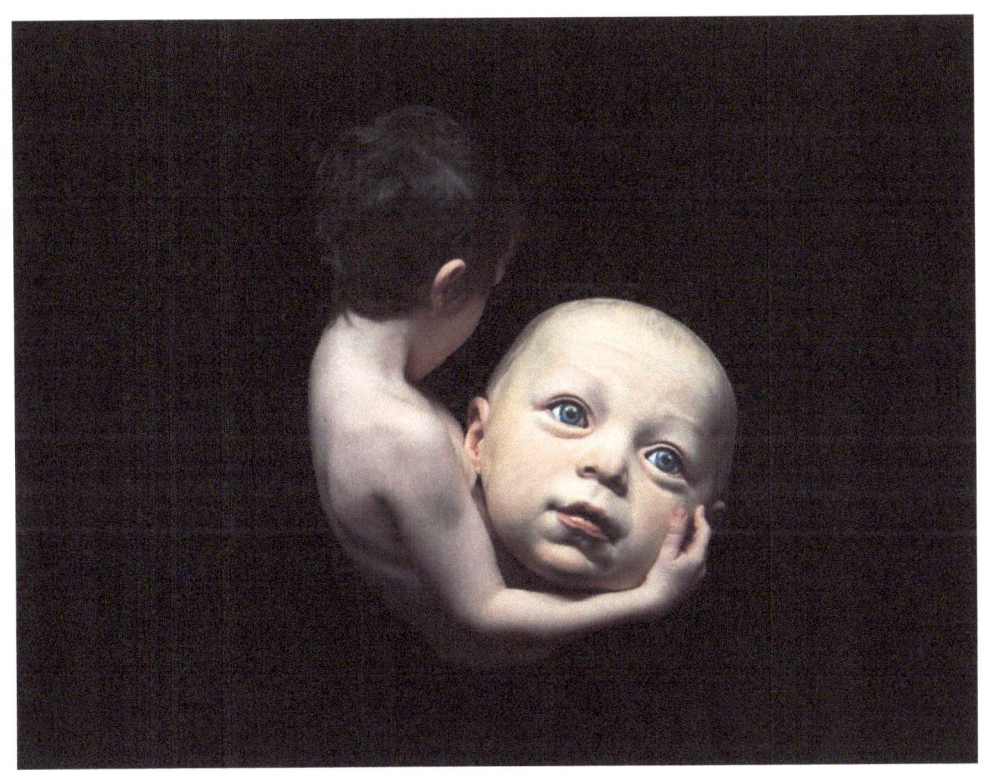

**BOY WITH BABY HEAD**
2007-8
digital C-print, mounted and framed
image 18 x 24 in., mounted and framed 26 x 31 in.
1/10 + a.p.

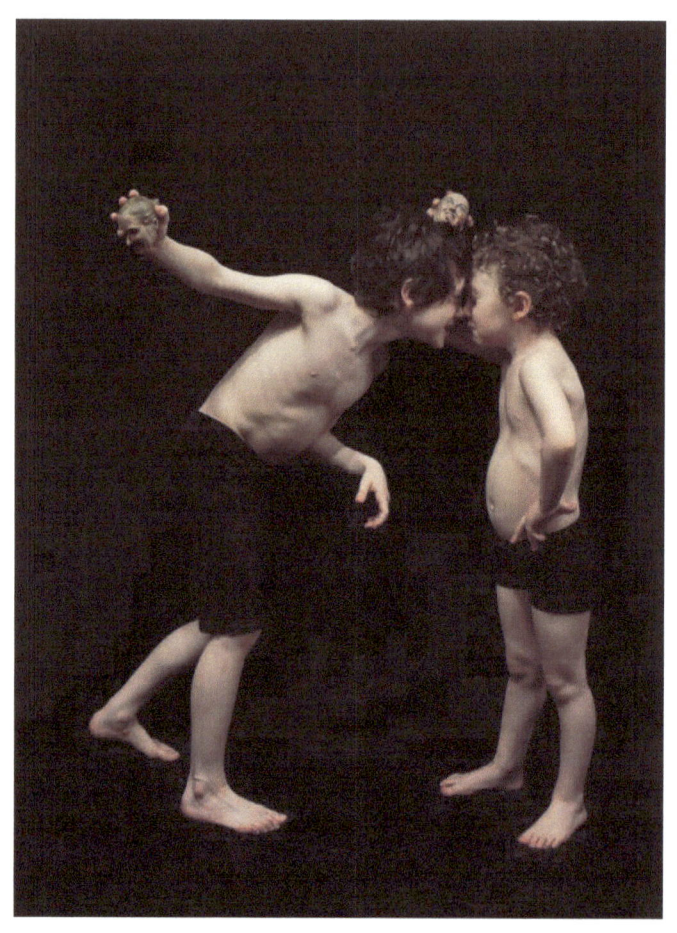

### *TWO BOYS WITH HEADS*
2011
digital c-print, mounted and framed
image is 24 x 18 in., mounted and framed: 31 x 26 in.
1/10 + a.p.

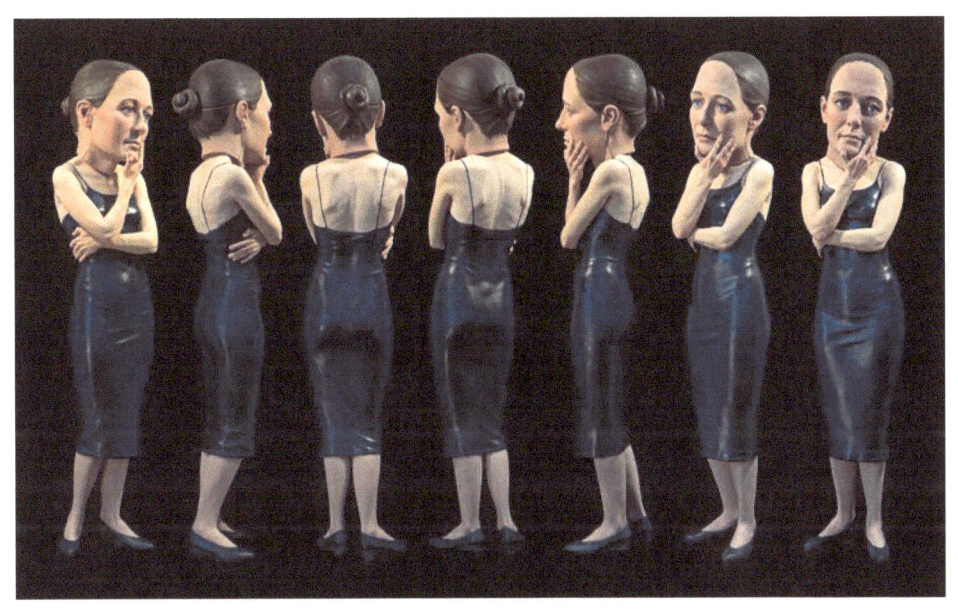

**SPECTATOR**
2004
polyester resin, oil paint
72 x 17 x 15 in.
a.p of an edition of three

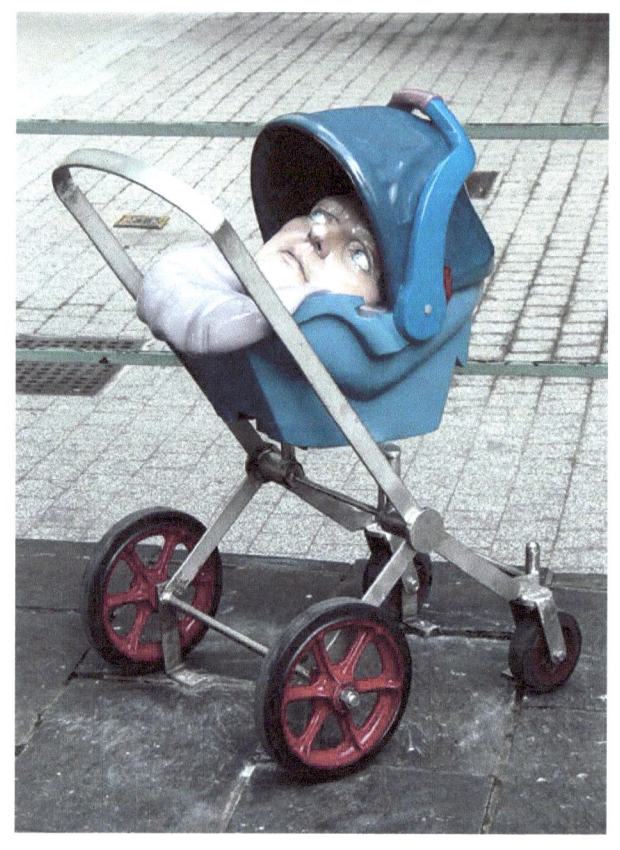

***STROLLER***
2004
polyester resin, automotive paint, stainless steel, cast iron, rubber
40 ½ x 34 x 26 in.

# D. DOMINICK LOMBARDI

For close to four decades D. Dominick Lombardi has dedicated much of his life to making and exhibiting paintings, drawings and mixed media sculptures that address the ever worsening state of the human condition.

Reviews of Lombardi's exhibitions have appeared in such publications as Sculpture, ARTnews, artnet, NY Art Beat, Time Out New York, Zing, O2 magazine (China), THE NEW YORK GAHO (cover and feature-Japan), Poetry and Thought (Japan), Skin and Ink and The New York Times.

Lombardi's art can be found in a number of collections including the Los Angeles County Museum of Art, Queens Museum of Art and The Housatonic Museum of art.

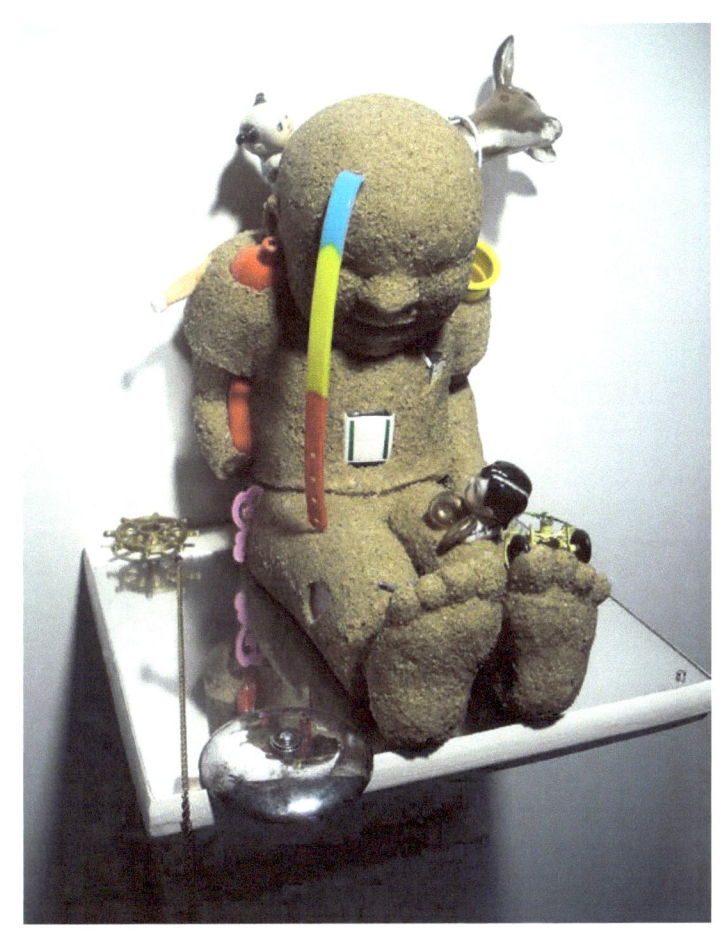

**URCHIN #48**
2013
sand, acrylic medium, objects and mirror
51 ½ x 12 x 12 in. (including wall mounted pedestal)

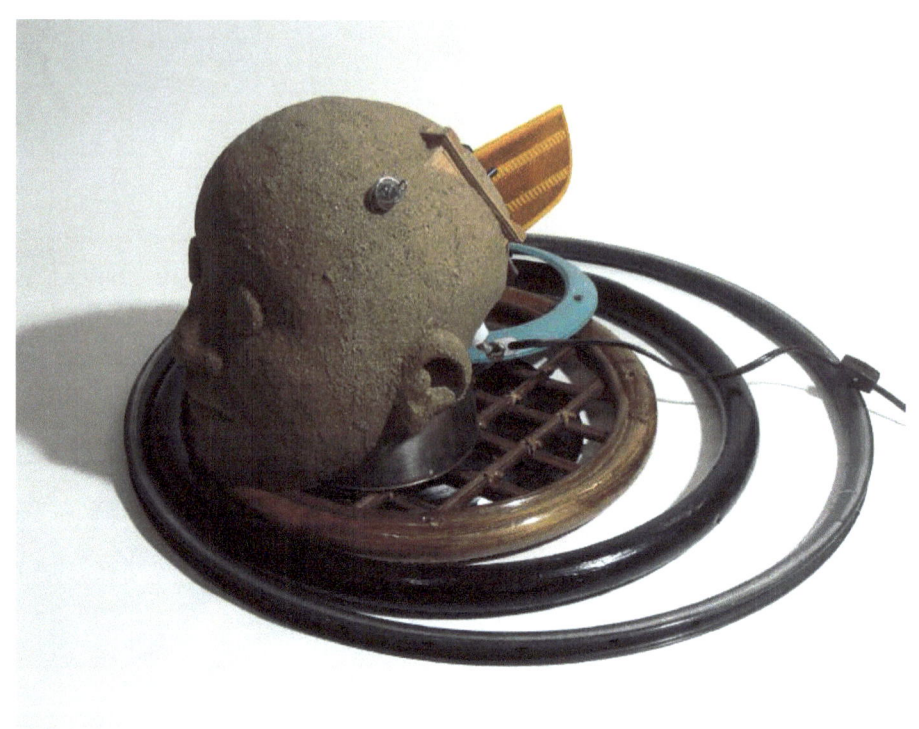

**_URCHIN #38_**
2012
sand, acrylic medium, objects and electric light
12 x 24 x 24 in.

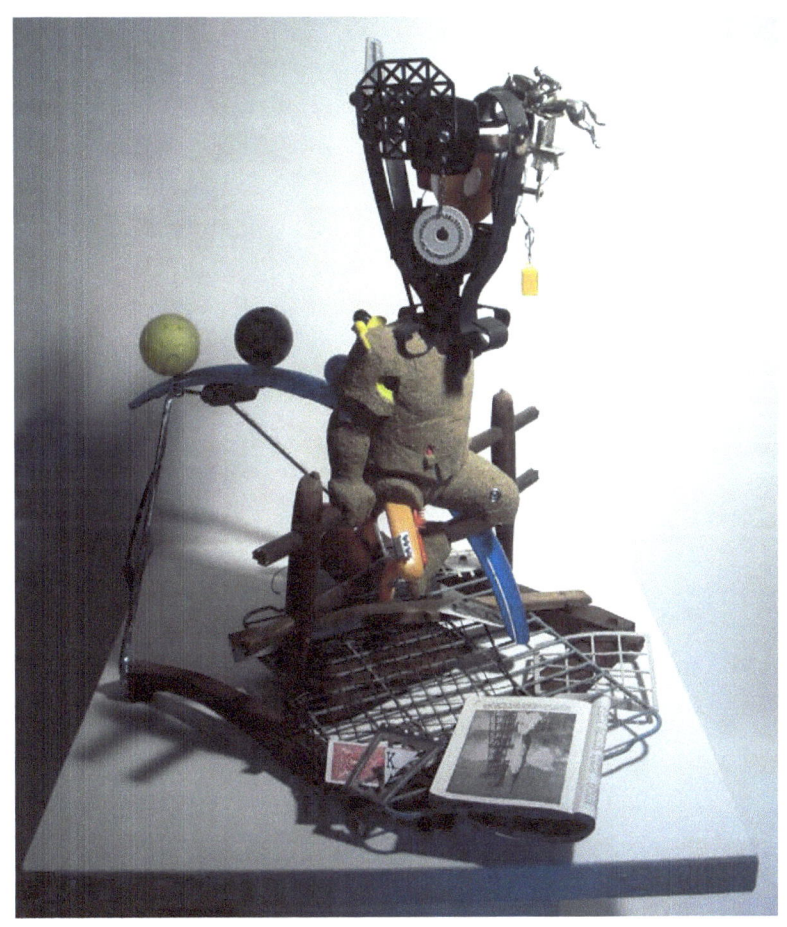

**URCHIN #36**
2011
sand, acrylic medium, objects and electric light
27 x 26 x 21 in.

# Esther Naor

Esther Naor was born in 1961 in Israel. She graduated from the department of Civil Engineering at Haifa Technion Institute, Israel, and the department of Computer Sciences at Tel Aviv University, Israel.

Following 12 years of a career in engineering and computers in the high-tech industry, she began art studies at the Midrasha Art School in Kfar Saba and at several artists' studios in Israel. Since the year 2001 she has been dedicating herself to art, working mainly in the mediums of sculpture, installation, photography, and video.

She lives and works in Israel.

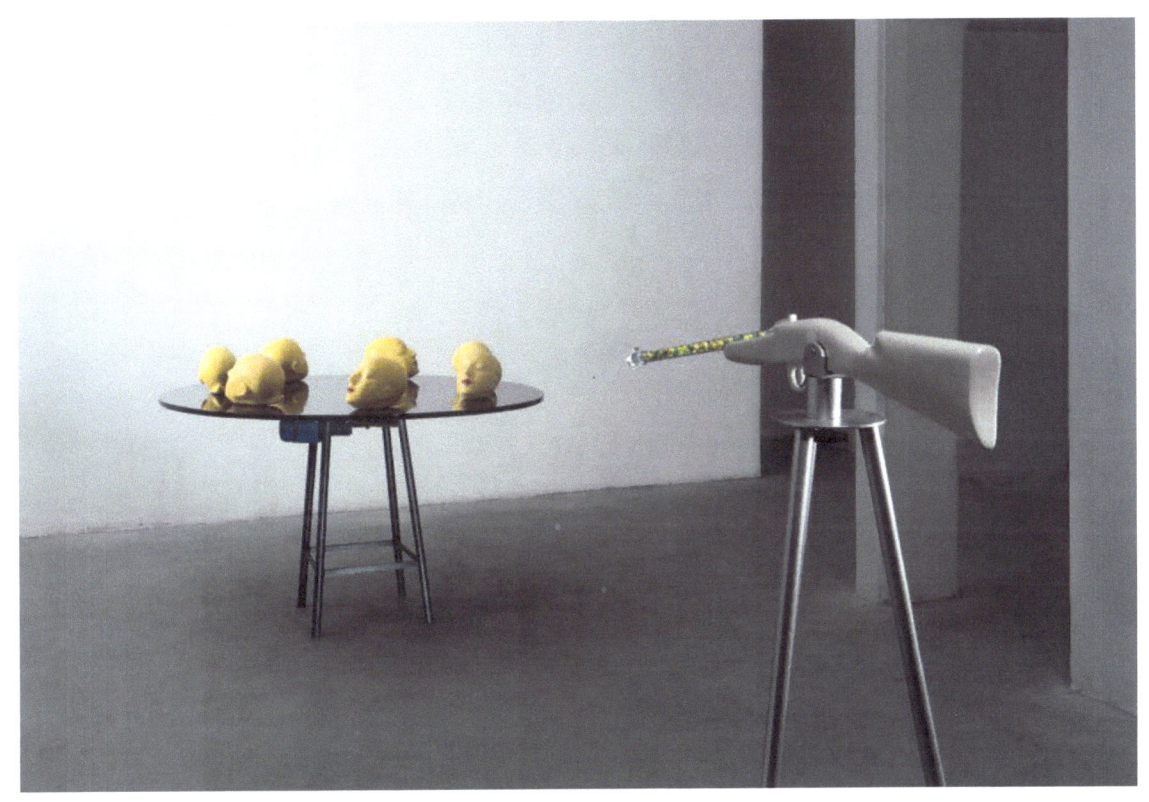

***BE A GOOD GIRL***
2012
mixed media
Variable dimensions

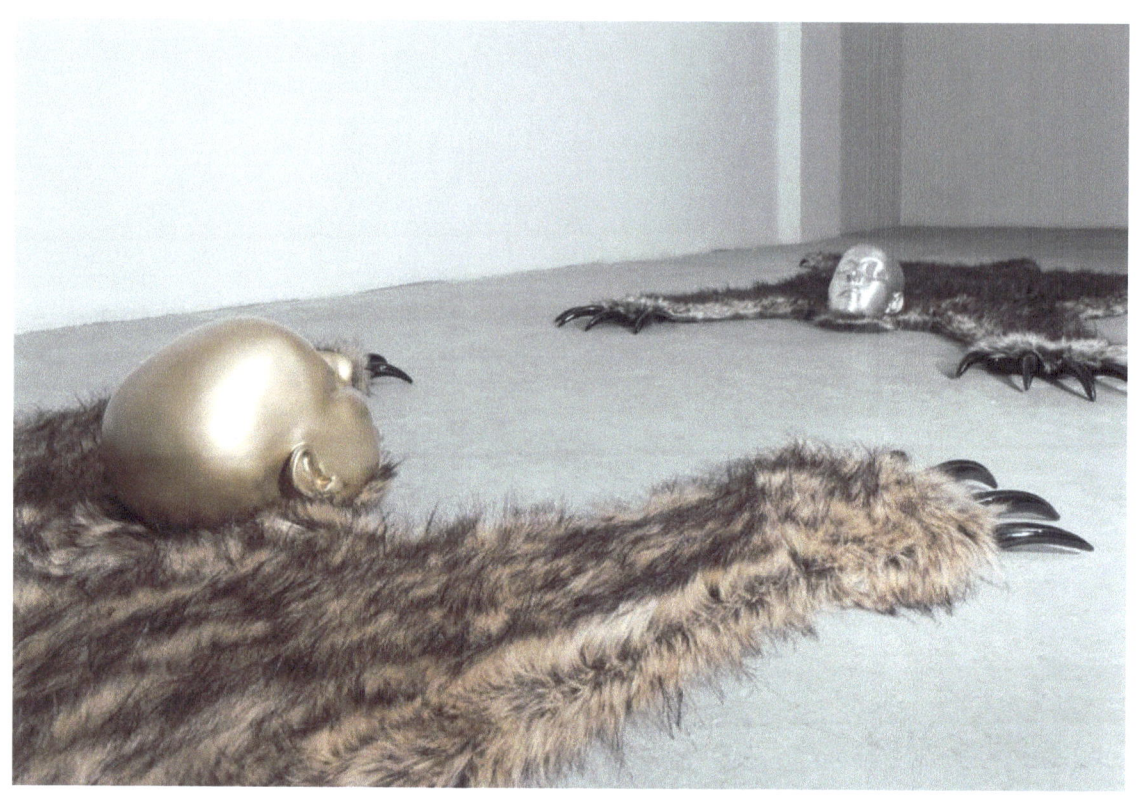

**QUEEN ESTHER 1 & 2**
2012
mixed media
7 ½ x 12 ¾ x 92 ½ in. each part

# Lena Viddo

Half Colombian, half Swedish painter, Lena Viddo grew up in and around Washington DC and later moved to New York City to pursue her passion for art. She received her BA in Illustration and Fine Art from F.I.T. State University of New York. She later attended the Polimoda in Florence, Italy where she studied Renaissance painting techniques. In 2011 Viddo represented USA at the Florence Biennale in December. This past fall she exhibited in "Bad For You" an exhibition curated by Beth Rudin Dewoody at Shizaru Gallery in London.

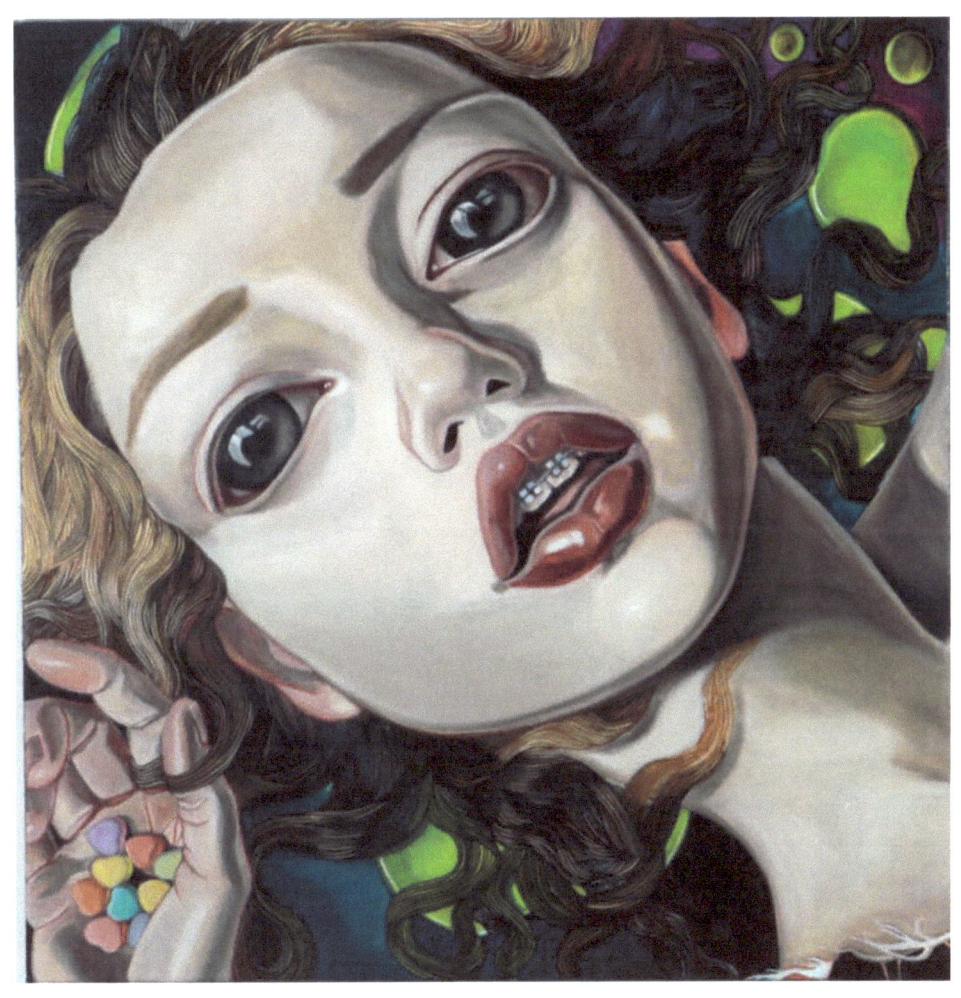

**HEART SHAPED BOX**
2012
oil on canvas
36 x 36 in.

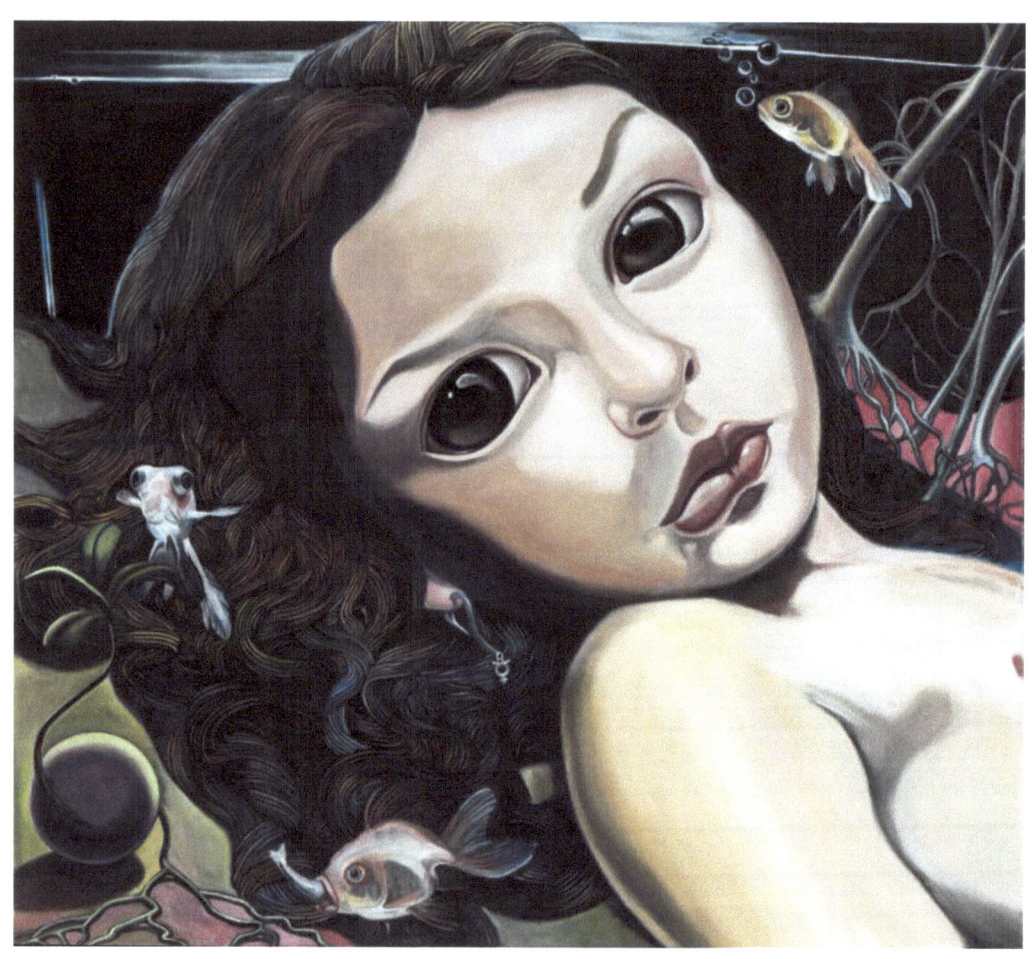

**OPHELIA**
2012
oil on canvas
36 x 40 in.

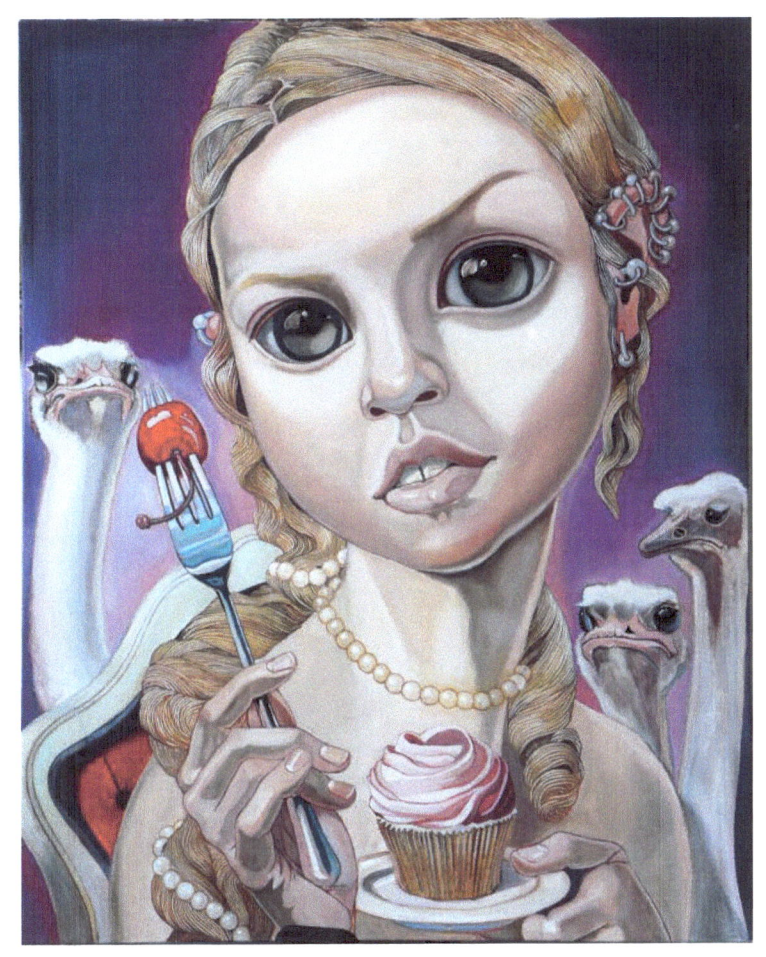

**_MADAME DEFICIT_**
2013
oil on canvas
44 x 36 in.

# CONTRIBUTORS

**Robert Curcio** | curcioprojects is a curator, writer, dealer, artist and exhibition management, and consultant to international art fairs. Recent curatorial projects and/or exhibition management include solo exhibitions of Kathleen Elliot, *Imaginary Botanicals* at the Tenri Cultural Institute, NYC and Nancy Friedemann *On the Margins of a Portrait* at The Gallery 1GAP. Art fairs include Pinta NYC, 2012, CONTEXTMiami, 2012 and Slick Paris, 2013. Curcio's profile of gallerist Annina Nosei appeared in Artvoices' spring 2013 issue. He was a co-founder and co-producer of the Scope Art Fairs.

Since 1978, **D. Dominick Lombardi** was and is the curator of numerous exhibitions in a variety of museums and galleries across the United States For the past eighteen years Lombardi's features and art criticisms have appeared in The New York Times, The Huffington Post, ARTslant, Art in Asia (S. Korea), Public Art and Ecology (China), Art Experience NYC, Sculpture, Sculpture Review, d'ART, Art Papers, Art Lies, ARTnews, & magazine, Art New England, NYARTS magazine and culturecatch.com among others.

# ACKNOWLEDGMENTS

As curators of HEAD, we want to thank all of the artists, as well as Freight + Volume, Claire Oliver and Galerie Richard, for kindly agreeing to lend the works and making this exhibition possible. We would also like to thank the director of BOSI Contemporary, Sandro Bosi and the gallery staff.

Thank you to Alacrán Tequila, Vibrant Rioja, and Tacos Gordos for the generous support.

Robert Curcio
D. Dominick Lombardi

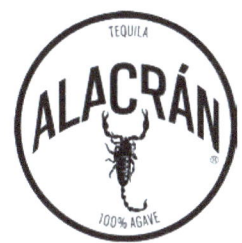

BOSI Contemporary was established by Sandro Bosi, an art dealer based in New York and London. Active in both primary and secondary markers, the gallery occupies the space at 48 Orchard Street (between Grand and Hester) and it focuses its attention on creating a dynamic space for artists and other art practioners to realize their vision and establish a platform for discourse that will nurture a thoughtful and creative community as well as attract new audiences.

International in scope, the gallery exhibits and communicates the work of both emerging and established artists, selected for their unique aesthetic language and fascinating vision. In addition, BOSI Contemporary annually organizes an exhibition dedicated to an artist of historical importance.

Published by BOSI Contemporary, on the occasion of the exhibition *HEAD* curated by Robert Curcio and D. Dominick Lombardi, on view from July 10 to August 11, 2013.

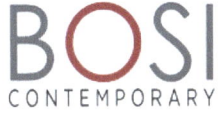

BOSI Contemporary
48 Orchard Street
New York, NY 10002
www.bosicontemporary.com

www.ingramcontent.com/pod-product-compliance
Lightning Source LLC
Chambersburg PA
CBHW051044180526
45172CB00002B/516